Data Sharing

Snowflake Special Edition

by Lawrence C. Miller

A Wiley Brand

Data Sharing For Dummies®, Snowflake Special Edition

Published by

John Wiley & Sons, Inc.

111 River St.

Hoboken, NJ 07030-5774

www.wiley.com

For general information on our other products and services, or how to create a custom For Dummies book for your business or organization, please contact our Business Development Department in the U.S. at 877-409-4177, contact info@dummies.biz, or visit www.wiley.com/go/custompub. For information about licensing the For Dummies brand for products or services, contact BrandedRights&Licenses@Wiley.com.

ISBN 978-1-119-49129-3 (pbk); ISBN 978-1-119-49127-9 (ebk)

Manufactured in the United States of America

C10007091_122018

Publisher's Acknowledgments

We're proud of this book and of the people who worked on it. Some of the people who helped bring this book to market include the following:

Project Editor: Martin V. Minner

Editorial Manager: Rev Mengle

Executive Editor: Steve Hayes

Business Development Representative: Karen Hattan

Production Editor: Siddique Shaik

Snowflake Review Team:
Michael Nixon, Vincent Morello, Matt Glickman, Robert Fehrmann, Marta Bright

Table of Contents

Introduction

Organizations inside an enterprise acquire crucial insight by analyzing data they share with each other. For example, finance teams need sales data to forecast future financial performance. Product management teams require marketing data to determine future products and services. Executive management needs up-to-the minute dashboards, fueled by data from many parts of the enterprise to make timely, data-driven business decisions.

Outside the enterprise, retailers share sales data with their vendors to manage inventory and supply chains. Software-as-a-service (SaaS) providers share the data they collect with their customers to provide them deeper insights into their business and other operational analytics. Healthcare providers securely share patient data with a multitude of vendors that provide ancillary products and with other business partners that analyze that data to help improve patient services. The list goes on and on.

Data has become more than something to collect and analyze. It's an asset that can be easily and securely made available inside and outside enterprises to streamline operations, to swiftly deliver more personalized customer experiences, and to open up new market opportunities. Data can also be monetized, creating a self-service data economy between an endless number of data providers and data consumers.

About This Book

Until recently, no technology has existed to share data across an enterprise — and beyond — without a significant amount of risk, cost, headache, and delay.

Welcome to *Data Sharing For Dummies,* Snowflake Special Edition, where you explore how modern data sharing enables any enterprise to share and receive live data, within minutes, in a governed and secure way. Modern data sharing allows an enterprise to easily and quickly forge one-to-one, one-to-many, and many-to-many relationships, to share data in new and imaginative ways that can dramatically reduce time to insight to a level never before possible.

Foolish Assumptions

I assume you are a business user who wants to share data or receive shared data. Or perhaps you are a data scientist needing access to massive data sets to train your model. Or, you may be a data engineer or data warehouse manager who must evaluate viable solutions for sharing data. Or, you may be an executive who wants to understand how data sharing can create new business opportunities. Whatever your objective, I assume it is very important to you to make timely decisions based on all available data.

Icons Used in This Book

Throughout this book, I occasionally use special icons to call attention to important information. Here's what to expect:

REMEMBER

This icon points out information you should commit to your non-volatile memory, your gray matter.

TECHNICAL STUFF

This icon explains the jargon beneath the jargon.

TIP

This icon points out useful nuggets of information and helpful advice.

WARNING

These alerts offer practical advice to help you avoid potentially costly or frustrating mistakes.

Beyond the Book

At the end of this book, if you're thinking, "Where can I learn more?" just go to www.snowflake.net to find out more about Snowflake and what they offer, obtain details about modern cloud data sharing, view webinars, get the scoop on upcoming events, and access documentation and other support. You can get in touch with them or even try their technology for free!

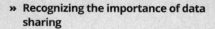

» Recognizing the importance of data sharing

» Exploring data sharing examples

» Understanding how organizations share data

» Taking advantage of data sharing opportunities

Chapter **1**

Getting Up to Speed on Data Sharing Basics

Every day, enterprises everywhere use data to track business results, make decisions, engage customers, define and create products, forecast trends, and more. Data is also a resource used and consumed between organizations, internal and external to one another, to collaborate on business plans, mutual initiatives, or joint opportunities.

There's no limit to how enterprises can engage and collaborate with data. However, data does not magically appear on the doorsteps, figuratively speaking, of an enterprise. It is generated at a place of origin and then distributed across the enterprise and analyzed to gain insights.

In this chapter, you learn about data sharing — what it is, why it matters, how and why enterprises share data, and what business opportunities data sharing can create.

What Is Data Sharing?

Data can originate from the many software applications an enterprise uses to run its business, from the constant activity of visitors engaging a website, from an Internet of Things (IoT) device attached to the refrigerator in your home, or to a sensor built into something as sophisticated as the jet engine of an airliner. There are potentially endless data-creating scenarios in the modern world. Market intelligence firm IDC has estimated that the world's total digital data created will increase to 180 zettabytes by 2025 (one zettabyte is equal to about one trillion gigabytes). Unfortunately, traditional data sharing methods require moving data, which is riddled with problems. Going forward it will be impractical, if not impossible, to share vast amounts of data in meaningful ways.

Furthermore, many enterprises have come to realize they could enhance their business operations if they had access to data outside their organizations. Enterprises also recognize it is not easy to access data they don't generate themselves. Thus, *data sharing* is the act of providing access to data between organizations inside the same enterprise, or between enterprises external to each other. The enterprise that shares its data is called a *data provider.* The enterprise that wants to use shared data is called the *data consumer.* Any enterprise can be a data provider, data consumer, or both.

Figure 1-1 shows how enterprises have traditionally shared data — by making a copy of the shared data and sending it to their data consumers. The data consumers then download the data to analyze or combine that data with their existing data for deeper insight into who their customers are, how efficiently their business operates, and into which new industries their business is heading.

But this process is slow, cumbersome, costly, and only allows for moving limited amounts of shared data. Figure 1-2 shows how modern data sharing happens without moving data. Instead, a data provider makes available live, read-only copies of data to its data consumers via modern cloud data sharing.

Traditional Data Sharing

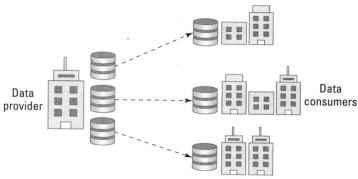

FIGURE 1-1: Traditional data sharing requires duplicating and moving data from a data provider to data consumers.

Modern Cloud Data Sharing

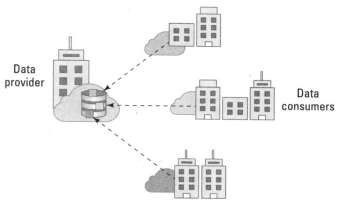

FIGURE 1-2: Modern cloud data sharing enables fast, live, secure, and governed data sharing without moving data.

TECHNICAL STUFF

A *data warehouse* is a type of database that contains a copy of an organization's data, which is used for analytical or reporting purposes. With a data warehouse, users can query the data to uncover trends, predict future behavior, and more. The data warehouse emerged because analyzing data stored in a an enterprise's primary data store, its database, would significantly impact performance. A database is designed for the real-time, rapid storage and retrieval of small sets of current data such as entering a customer name, recording a sale, and recording accounting activity of that sale.

PORTAL FOR JOB SEEKERS IMPROVES 300 PERCENT

Snagajob's mobile sourcing and hiring tools connect 75 million registered hourly workers to Snagajob's business subscribers, which represent 300,000 employer locations.

Snagajob had a need to share its data from its data warehouse with an external marketing analytics firm. The firm then used the data to reach out to Snagajob's business clients to execute targeted re-engagement campaigns on behalf of Snagajob. This relationship allowed Snagajob to avoid in-house labor costs associated with this marketing function.

To share its data, Snagajob routinely had to implement time-consuming steps that included:

- Identifying the database elements to be shared
- Extracting the data set with a client tool
- Compressing and encrypting the data in order to email it
- Emailing the file to the marketing partner

After the external marketing firm received the file, it would execute the same time-consuming steps in reverse, with the additional steps of building a database table to ingest the data and then importing the data into its target database.

Snagajob turned to a modern, built-for-the-cloud data warehouse that could operate as an extremely scalable data warehouse but also be its platform for data sharing. All Snagajob had to do was create a "share" that enabled its marketing partner to receive live, secure, and instantaneous access to the tables and views Snagajob shared. The marketing partner could then execute the email campaign with data provided that was always accurate and recent, because the partner always accesses a read-only version of Snagajob's latest data. All of this took place in a matter of minutes without any data movement.

Performance, reliability, and agility were dramatically increased, allowing Snagajob to reduce the implementation time to share data from several days to just a few hours. Snagajob saved 300 percent on costs and was able to operate much more quickly, which improved its industry competitiveness.

Data Sharing Examples

As explained earlier, the portion of data that exists outside an enterprise will grow exponentially. Whether from IoT data or from any other form of external data, when combined with an organization's own internal data, insights never before possible will reveal themselves.

Here are just a few of the new business opportunities that modern cloud data sharing makes possible:

>> **Data sharing to eliminate data silos:** Develop a single source of truth for all your internal data and sharing it among thousands of data consumers across hundreds of business units within a single enterprise.

>> **Data sharing for business efficiencies:** Share live data with your business partners to optimize costs, streamline operations, and provide superior customer service.

>> **Data sharing as a product:** Provide live and direct access to slices of your data as a monetized service so your data consumers can enrich their own existing data.

>> **Data sharing as a product differentiator:** Software-as-a-service (SaaS) providers can offer direct access to the petabytes of data generated from their business-to-business (B2B) subscribers' activity. Those subscribers can then perform deeper analysis on more of their data — analysis that was previously unavailable to them.

Capitalizing on these opportunities requires data sharing capabilities with uncommon speed, power, security, governance, and simplicity. These capabilities are not available with traditional data sharing methods.

How Organizations Share Data

Traditional approaches require laborious efforts to stitch together a patchwork of disparate tasks to share and move data. These processes are costly, create manual overhead, and limit how much data an organization can actually share:

>> **Email:** A data file is emailed from provider to consumer.

>> **File Transfer Protocol (FTP):** Data files are shared and downloaded between two computers or via the Internet.

>> **Extract, transfer, load (ETL) software:** ETL software extracts data from the provider's database, transforms the data, and then loads it into the consumer's database.

>> **Online file sharing services:** These are similar to FTP, but sharing and downloading data files takes place via Internet file transfer only.

>> **Cloud storage:** The provider stores data in the cloud and provides the consumer with credentials for accessing it.

>> **Application programming interfaces (APIs):** An API is used to initiate and manage the data transfer.

But imagine the possibilities of having on-demand access to ready-to-use, live data so you could make immediate use of that data inside a secure, governed environment.

Exploring Data Sharing Possibilities

With modern data sharing, the possibilities are practically endless. So, why might an organization explore new data sharing opportunities? Here are a few compelling reasons:

>> **Improve the customer experience.** Delivering targeted business or retail offerings with personalized marketing campaigns in a highly competitive, digital market requires a deeper understanding of your customers, competitors, and industry trends. The primary path to gain this understanding involves acquiring data you don't already have in order to reveal what you don't already know.

>> **Streamline your business.** Easily sharing data across the multitude of organizations that comprise your enterprise, and with your business partners, creates a single source of truth, which could save billions of dollars by reconciling the most minor data inconsistences. Your enterprise also gains the insight to make data-driven business decisions.

>> **Create new business assets from data.** Some data within a data provider will be just as valuable to thousands of external, non-competing data consumers. All of this can happen through an effortless, self-serving business model thanks to the simplicity of sharing any part of a modern, cloud data warehouse that offers modern data sharing.

Chapter **2**

Understanding Traditional Data Sharing Challenges

n this chapter, you learn about the many limitations of traditional data sharing methods and technologies.

Addressing a Multi-Faceted Problem

If you anticipate sharing data with tens, hundreds, or even thousands of internal or external data consumers — each of which has unique data sharing requirements — how can you easily support this challenge? How do you support growth without constantly building more storage clusters, managing complex software, and suffering through prolonged latencies and performance penalties — all without creating inconsistencies by sharing stale copies of data? Simply put, the traditional data warehouse platforms of today were not built to support the constant need to share data in real time.

To understand the magnitude of the challenges associated with traditional data sharing, consider the pros and cons of common approaches (shown in Table 2-1) that a company would encounter, for example, when sharing data with a third-party service provider or another external enterprise such as a business partner.

TABLE 2-1 Pros and cons of traditional data sharing approaches

Data Sharing Approach	Pros	Cons
Email	• Pervasive and ubiquitous • Infrastructure in place • Easy to compose an email and attach a file	• Not conducive for large data sets from relational databases (can't scale) • Limited size of attached files (less than 25MB) requires large data sets to be deconstructed and zipped • Limited network bandwidth, which results in slow data transmission • Not secure, requiring custom encryption • Mirror effort required on recipients' end (receive, decrypt, reconstruct data, and so on)
Extract, transfer, load (ETL) software	• Large availability of well-established ETL software solutions • Purpose-built to extract data from a database or data source and transform the data for loading into a target database • Good for bulk and complex data movement and transformations	• Latency emerges when data changes • Expensive software, costing up to tens of thousands of dollars • Complex, requiring specialized skills to integrate and deploy with a data warehouse • Can take months to implement • Change management and schema evolution can be difficult

Data Sharing Approach	Pros	Cons
Online file sharing services	• High availability of services • Generally easy to use	• Better suited for sharing flat files, not relational database objects • Data is not ready to use (ready to analyze) • Risk associated with data inconsistencies when the original copy of the data changes
Cloud storage	• Numerous services available from large cloud storage providers	• Less than optimal performance when querying directly from cloud storage • Change management and schema evolution difficult, requiring separate metadata management process • Risk exposure when data changes • Complete SQL data manipulation language (DML) semantics (such as UPDATE and INSERT) may not be supported
Application programming interfaces (APIs)	• Numerous APIs available • Wide variety of use cases • Programmatic implementation relieves some manual effort	• Data movement is required, creating risks for failed transfers • APIs process data in small amounts, creating bottlenecks for large data volumes • Performance is directly affected by available bandwidth, requiring high costs for higher bandwidths

(continued)

TABLE 2-1 *(continued)*

Data Sharing Approach	Pros	Cons
File transfer protocol (FTP) — (see Figure 2-1)	• Well-known and long-established protocol • Availability of a wide range of FTP client software and services	• Schema changes require a great deal of lead time • Must acquire FTP client software, server, and/or service • FTP account admin setup and overhead required • Large data sets must be deconstructed and broken down in size to facilitate faster data transfers • Not natively secure; requires custom encryption scripting or secure service • Mirror effort required on recipients' end (receive, decrypt, reconstruct data) • Efforts must be repeated with each new update to a shared data set

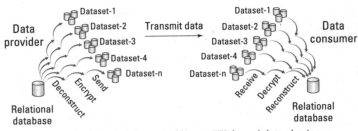

FIGURE 2-1: Multiple steps of a typical legacy FTP-based data sharing workflow.

Conventional Data Sharing: Time-to-Value Delays

Conventional data sharing methods can create other challenges that cause more delays and require more assistance from your IT teams, including:

>> **Handling increased data size:** The shared data set is often much larger than originally scoped, which creates problems with the data extraction process. You'll likely need a scripting language to automate the breakdown and extraction process, which may require additional IT assistance. The reverse process must also occur for data consumers.

>> **Decrypting sensitive data:** If the data set includes sensitive information, the output files will likely need to be encrypted, masked, or redacted, which may require additional IT assistance. If the data set is encrypted, encryption keys must be securely shared between the parties via a separate process, and the data consumer must decrypt the shared data.

>> **Changing file formats and schema:** It may be necessary to change the file format multiple times if additional database attributes must be shared. When table attributes change on the data provider's end, a corresponding change must also occur on the data consumer's end.

The accumulation of all these steps results in slow and painful processes for both data providers and consumers. All of this must happen *before* any attempt to analyze and develop insights from the data, which creates time-to-value delays.

Usually, the delays and difficulty don't end with just the transfer effort. For example:

>> **Sharing data in real time:** More IT assistance is needed if the data set could be shared in a more real-time fashion, rather than being sent only once per night.

>> **Cleaning data:** The import process has problems and the data isn't as clean as anticipated. For example, the data extraction may contain special characters that should have been disregarded. This means the data provider must build more sophisticated data extraction processes, resulting in more IT assistance, costs, and delays.

To protect against failures during the file transfer process, on either the extraction and/or import side, both the data provider and data consumer must incorporate special software code or scripts to monitor the transfer and automatically restart the process in the event of failure. This means greater effort and longer delays to develop insights and derive value from data.

LOCALYTICS: SPEEDING ACCESS TO DATA FROM BILLIONS OF DEVICES

Localytics is a Boston-based company that provides a mobile engagement platform used in more than 37,000 apps on more than 2.7 billion mobile devices worldwide. Localytics gives hundreds of the world's top brands insights about their mobile users and the tools to engage with those users.

Localytics uses modern data sharing to provide its customers with access to Localytics' data without exporting that data, solving one of the biggest data challenges marketers face. Previously, users had to connect different sources of customer data from customer relationship management (CRM) systems, business intelligence (BI) tools, mobile analytics, and other sources. Data was often exported and copied into other platforms, manipulated, and further analyzed. The process produced multiple copies of the data living in many places, increasing costs and complexity, and producing inconsistent results.

ETL eliminated

Localytics removed the burden of cumbersome ETL efforts to make data directly accessible through modern data sharing, creating a much more efficient and reliable way to manage and understand customer data. Specifically, Localytics employs secure, permissions-based access to enable customers to work with session, event, and profile data from Localytics and run their own queries and custom reports against that data. Customers can also use popular BI tools to analyze their data.

Data latency reduced from three hours to three minutes

Localytics stores all its data in a modern cloud data warehouse, augmented with modern data sharing. Instant sharing of live data with Localytics' customers eliminated a previous data latency of three hours. With modern data sharing, real-time data is ready to query in about three minutes. Customers don't need to expend effort to use the data, which is filtered through live, secure, governed, and permissions-based sharing.

"Customers immediately saw modern data sharing as potentially eliminating their ETL processes," Localytics Director of Engineering Michael Klos said. "That's important because they have overburdened data teams. Our customers are happy because our data sharing solution saves them time and effort."

Computing Complexity Challenges

Traditional options to share data also require scaling complex computing platforms to share even small slices of data. Complexity adds burdens and requires extra resources, including infrastructure costs — internally and externally.

The goal should be effortless sharing of limitless amounts of data with internal and external organizations, including your business partners, for collaboration and business planning. If your business model is focused on monetizing your data, you'll want the same level of effortless sharing to distribute data to as many data consumers as possible, with individualized, self-service access and security as needed.

WARNING

If you think cloud storage is the answer, think again. Sharing data using a basic cloud storage service is inefficient. It won't provide the ability for you or your data consumers to query the data in a high-performance manner or ensure data consistency. A Hadoop computing platform is not the answer either because of its inherent complexities and complications.

Conventional Data Sharing: Business Pain Points

Cumbersome and complex data sharing methods combined with costly and inflexible computing platforms produce headaches for organizations that need to collaborate on data. In addition, the processing overhead required to extract data from a traditional data warehouse and transfer that data to other organizations delays the value shared data provides. Additionally, every time data changes, data extraction and transfer processes must be repeated because shared data is always a static version and becomes stale immediately.

Within an organization

Data sharing scenarios within an organization include:

>> Sales groups share data with finance groups to track sales and revenue to forecast an organization's performance.

>> Marketing teams monitor and analyze customer data to predict behavior and align demand generation programs.

When functional groups within an organization cannot share data effectively, data silos result, and business collaboration suffers. Each group will maintain its own data warehouse or *data mart* — a copy of some of the data from the corporate data warehouse. Data silo and data mart sprawl ensue and create unnecessary burdens for IT and data warehouse teams.

Business-to-business (B2B)

Some examples of B2B data sharing scenarios include:

>> A hotel booking website shares reservation patterns and trends with hotel properties to develop promotional and pricing programs.

>> A grocery chain provides store sales data to suppliers to ensure shelves are adequately stocked to meet demand.

>> Retailers share in-store sales data to fashion merchandising so the hottest trends are always available.

Whether sharing data to other external organizations or receiving shared data from other organizations, if enterprises cannot collaborate on data they are less efficient and run the risk of operating at a higher cost and lower productivity.

Monetizing data

An example of monetizing shared data is a data service company that gathers mobile phone location information and usage data and then shares the information with advertising agencies and marketing groups so they can execute highly targeted campaigns to specific consumers.

The inability to extract insight from data quickly is an inhibitor to maximizing the commercial value from data. Data consumers encounter delays in developing insights, which can lead to dissatisfaction with the data provider. Furthermore, because common methods to share data can't incorporate changes immediately, data consumers risk executing analytics on incomplete data. This can lead to less accurate analytics or faulty conclusions for business decisions.

Chapter **3**

Recognizing the Business Value of Sharing Data

I n this chapter, you learn how data sharing methods have evolved in business, why data sharing is critical to any business, how businesses share data internally and externally, and how the cloud and software-as-a-service (SaaS) change the data sharing model.

Looking Back at the Early Days of Data Sharing

Understanding the business value of data sharing today requires a historical perspective. Not long ago, it was considered the norm for organizations to host and support multiple business applications within their own data centers. There would be an application for finance, another for marketing, others for sales, human resources, operations, and so on. Just ten years ago, large companies would host and run hundreds of business applications from their own data centers.

Each of these applications would also have an associated database. These databases were not optimized for analytics and did not share data between applications. In order to analyze this data, each business unit in charge of a database would have to extract, transform, and load (ETL) the data into its own *data mart,* which is a smaller, stand-alone version of a data warehouse. Then, to develop business intelligence across an organization or to execute analytics against company-wide data, data would have to be sent through the ETL process from the individual data marts into a central data warehouse. This data would then be prepared for analytics. The entire process was slow and cumbersome. Data formats varied across the applications, requiring further modeling and transformation into a new data warehouse. But, at least you had access to the data because it was in your own data center.

The bottom line is that no company survives without some level of internal data sharing.

REMEMBER

The Business Value of Data Sharing for Organizations

Data sharing across and beyond an organization consists of four basic work flows:

>> **Across lines of business (LOBs):** Sharing data between organizations within the same enterprise

>> **Between enterprises:** Outbound data sharing to another, separate enterprise to benefit your business

>> **Between enterprises:** Receiving inbound data shared from another enterprise to benefit your business

>> **Monetizing data:** Sharing live data as a service so data consumers can enrich their own, existing data

Across LOBs and groups within the same enterprise

Within the same enterprise, organizations depend on email, spreadsheets, shared network drives, application programming interfaces (APIs), and other methods for communicating and for sharing data. Along with facilitating day-to-day business, sharing data across an enterprise enables and fosters increased levels of business intelligence and drives timely and informed business decisions.

But within an enterprise, data is often locked in silos. Mergers or acquisitions, firewall restrictions, or other business or technology barriers often restrict an enterprise from easily sharing data across its organizations. These physical or logical separations of infrastructure can prevent two or more organizations from accessing all available data within an enterprise to deliver all-inclusive, data-driven insights. These data silos emerge when an enterprise relies on a traditional, on-premises data warehouse or a traditional data warehouse ported to the cloud.

Between enterprises: Outbound data sharing

External data sharing takes place all the time between different companies. It can be a vendor-supplier relationship, a partner relationship, a developer-producer relationship, or any number of other business relationships that require two or more enterprises to collaborate with data to drive business. In Figure 3-1, the primary organization is sharing data, outbound, to the partner organization.

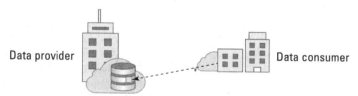

Outbound Modern Data Sharing

Data provider   Data consumer

FIGURE 3-1: An enterprise, acting as the data provider, shares data with its supplier, the data consumer.

For example, in a vendor-supplier relationship with data sharing, a supplier knows in advance when to replenish the stock of a particular item. Well-managed inventory also prevents overstocking, minimizing the need to significantly reduce prices, which can reduce a company's margin.

Between enterprises: Inbound data sharing

Increasingly, enterprises engage outside service companies. These contracted service companies can specialize in logistics, shipping, marketing services, or sales operations, just to name a few. For example, a large retailer would collect massive amounts of demographic data about its target customers. The retailer would then share this data as a data provider to a data analytics company.

From there, the analytics company would analyze the data for the retailer. It would then provide the analysis back to the retailer in the form of an inbound data share, as shown in Figure 3-2.

Inbound Modern Data Sharing

FIGURE 3-2: The enterprise is the data consumer, accessing the data from its outside data analytics vendor, which is the data provider.

In other scenarios, the enterprise contracts a service provider to perform a function the enterprise chooses not to perform in-house. In turn, the service provider generates data as a result of that service — data that belongs to its enterprise customer. With inbound data sharing between organizations, the data generated by the service provider is shared with its enterprise customer. The enterprise customer then executes additional analytics to develop deeper insights and value from additional data generated outside its data center but within its business ecosystem.

Monetizing data

Data can also take on more significance today than just day-to-day collaboration. Data is a business asset — a currency. As such, data can offer different types of value depending on the organization that wants to consume that data. Thus, as with any asset, data has value. To monetize the value of its data, a provider can sell data to consumers that can use the data to advance their own business objectives (see Figure 3-3).

Monetized Cloud Data Sharing

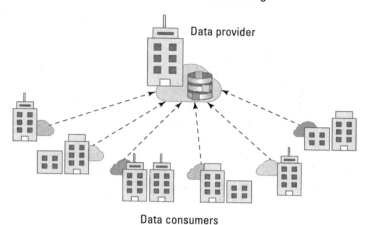

FIGURE 3-3: An enterprise data provider creates new revenue opportunities by sharing data with other enterprises, acting as data consumers.

With shared data, data consumers can use data without having to capture and collect it themselves. They can benefit directly from analyzing that data or combining it with other data to enhance its value.

But harnessing the value of data — either for consumption, mass collaboration, or value-added business opportunities — requires an easy method for enabling data access without actually moving the data. Traditional data sharing methods are too costly, risky, and labor intensive. Monetizing data requires the ability to easily and affordably create a secure, self-service business model to share data between data providers and data consumers.

GAMING PLATFORM SHARES DATA TO HELP SERVE 90 MILLION GAMERS

PlayFab provides back-end services and data logistics for its game studio customers that serve 75 million monthly average gamers and 15 million daily average gamers. PlayFab shares player data for each game with each respective game studio. PlayFab also anonymizes

(continued)

(continued)

aggregated data across all studios and shares those results with all its game studio customers.

On the receiving end of the shared data, game studios optimize games based on the shared player data from PlayFab. They may run A/B tests to uncover the best designs and tune games to the right level of difficulty and revenue. Additionally, game studios deploy predictive models on the shared data to forecast attrition, virality, and lifetime value.

Because data is the lifeblood of a modern game, the need for high-quality, real-time data goes well beyond reporting simple vanity metrics such as daily or monthly usage, retention, and average revenue per user (ARPU). To identify problems, test hypotheses, and ultimately improve games, there is no substitute for gathering, storing, and quickly analyzing large quantities of raw data from gaming activity.

When gathering data, and sharing it with game studios, PlayFab regularly encountered challenges such as:

- Capturing the right data, the first time
- Getting data from client devices and moving it into the data pipeline
- Managing constantly changing data schemas driven by new game data events
- Reducing soaring costs due to moving and transferring high volumes of game data

To solve these challenges, PlayFab adopted a modern, cloud-built data warehouse.

Although data events are specific to individual games, PlayFab does not need to know the schema ahead of time. This is enabled by the full SQL and direct JSON support of the modern cloud data warehouse. Raw data is loaded directly into the warehouse's modern data sharing platform with no transformation needed, which then provides the most accurate representation of the data possible. Reports, among other things, are generated with high reliability.

With modern data sharing, PlayFab sets up secure, governed, and live views of the data with each game studio under a straightforward, self-service business model. This method avoids ETL entirely. Secure and governed views guarantee that each game studio's data is truly isolated and game designers get direct access to a direct feed of live game data, without any custom import required.

Chapter **4**

Enabling Live Data Sharing with a Modern Cloud Data Warehouse Architecture

I n this chapter, you learn how a modern, built-for-the-cloud data warehouse architecture helps data providers and data consumers overcome traditional data sharing challenges. You also learn how to use real-time data sharing from inside a modern cloud data warehouse environment to quickly and easily enable secure and governed views of live data for your data consumers.

Modern Data Sharing: Out with the Old, in with the New

As discussed in Chapter 2, data sharing is a multi-faceted challenge. But traditional methods of data sharing fundamentally address only one part of the challenge — providing data consumers access to a provider's data. Although traditional data warehouses and *data lakes* (repositories that store massive amounts raw data until needed for analysis) were designed to make data usable, their underlying architectures are not capable of modern data sharing — providing data access to data consumers without having to move the provider's data.

Burdens of old methods of data sharing

Traditional data sharing is slow, and it reduces an enterprise's ability to execute quickly. In addition, a lack of security and governance, among other things, means traditional data warehouses and data lake architectures cannot support unlimited concurrent access by data consumers or real-time data changes by data providers without cumbersome unloading and transferring of data, as shown in Figure 4-1. This puts data consumers at risk of operating on stale (static) data.

Traditional Data Sharing Method

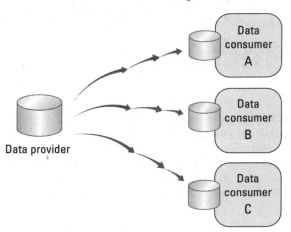

FIGURE 4-1: Traditional data sharing requires cumbersome, multi-step processes by data providers to deconstruct, encrypt, and send data. For data consumers, they must perform the reverse process on the shared data.

The lack of a comprehensive solution creates a struggle for data providers and consumers to easily share data and ensure data consistency. These barriers also limit the ability to monetize data and create new business opportunities.

Opportunities with modern data sharing

With modern data sharing inside a modern, cloud-built data warehouse, in a matter of minutes, you (as a data provider) can enable live access to any of your data stored in your data warehouse for any number of data consumers, inside or outside your organization. You can share data across internal business units, with business partners across your ecosystem, and with enterprises external to your organization to easily support richer analytics, data-driven initiatives, new business models, and new revenue streams. Figure 4-2 shows the benefits and opportunities modern data sharing provides.

FIGURE 4-2: Modern cloud data sharing allows enterprises to dramatically improve many areas of their business.

With modern data sharing, ready-to-use data is immediately available in real time. In a modern cloud data warehouse architecture, query speeds on shared data are exponentially faster and fortified with limitless storage and compute resources.

Modern data sharing extends the architecture and functionality of the modern cloud data warehouse as a platform to share data. Enterprises of any size can grant read-only access to their live, ready-to-use data (structured and semi-structured) in a secure and governed environment. Data consumers can then choose to combine (JOIN) data from other organizations to augment and deepen their data analytics.

REMEMBER

Only the scalability, elasticity, and flexibility of a multi-tenant cloud data warehouse-as-a-service makes it possible to store data from diverse sources and share that data among a large number of data consumers without contention or competition for resources.

Making data sharing easy

Enterprises can realize the business benefits of modern cloud data sharing thanks to the architecture of a cloud–built data warehouse, which

>> **Eliminates movement and copying of data:** Modern data sharing offers direct, real-time access to live data in a secure, managed, and controlled environment.

>> **Provides ready-to-use data:** Data consumers get the full capabilities of a data warehouse, allowing them to analyze shared data within minutes. They can combine shared data with their own data. Security, governance, data schema, and metadata are all provided within the modern data warehouse.

>> **Enables data sharing without added costs:** Modern data sharing eliminates the duplicative costs of building the infrastructure needed to store shared data, since data consumers view the shared data directly from the data provider without any copying or movement of data.

>> **Enables data sharing with unlimited data providers and consumers:** Unlike traditional data warehouses that have limited ability to support multiple user groups accessing and analyzing the same data, a modern cloud data warehouse can serve an unlimited number of data providers and consumers, with full transactional integrity and data consistency.

TIP

Modern cloud data sharing eliminates the delays, cost, and friction of existing methods, which provide only primitive mechanisms for data publishing, access, and control. Modern data sharing is built on three key architectural innovations:

>> Decoupling of storage and compute

>> Multi-tenant metadata, security, and transactional management

>> Unlimited concurrency

Decoupling of storage, compute, and services

The separation of storage and compute resources is a fundamental part of a modern data sharing architecture, as shown in Figure 4-3. All data is stored, in optimized form and without any loss of data fidelity, in the cloud. A single copy of the data stored in a modern cloud data warehouse — a single source of truth — can be accessed concurrently by any number of independent compute clusters, enabling an organization to perform any number of internal workloads, such as analytics.

The Cloud-built Data Warehouse

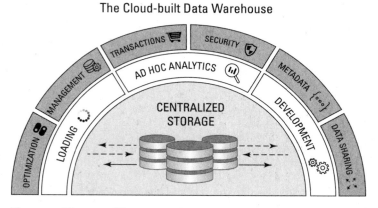

☐ Services ☐ Compute ☐ Storage

FIGURE 4-3: A modern data sharing architecture built for the cloud with storage, compute, and services completely separate from each other.

TIP

Decoupling of storage and compute is also critical for sharing data. It enables data consumers to directly access shared data, using their own data warehouse compute power. But data consumers don't pay for storage costs (because the shared data doesn't move), and the data provider doesn't pay for any of the compute that a data consumer uses to analyze shared data.

Multi-tenant metadata and transaction management

Making shared data usable requires access to data and coordination across all data consumers to ensure consistency, security, and performance.

The services layer is a key part of a modern data sharing architecture. Global metadata, transactions, and security are all managed from here, making the services layer the control tower that tracks, logs, and directs access to data for every database element and object contained within the data warehouse, as shown in Figure 4-4.

Modern Data Sharing Architecture

FIGURE 4-4: Metadata in a modern data sharing architecture enables access to live data between a data provider and data consumer, without moving data.

Additionally, the services layer provides transactional consistency across all data providers and data consumers, ensuring that all data users see a consistent view of the data that is always live and up to date. A data provider can update shared data in real time. Likewise, after transactions are committed, all data consumers can view the data provider's updates and immediately query the shared data at the same time — all with transactional, ACID-based consistency.

ACID is a consistency model that defines a set of properties to ensure transactions in a relational database are valid, even in the event of multi-statement transactions and processing errors, as well as power failures and crashes. The properties of ACID are:

TECHNICAL STUFF

>> **Atomicity ("all or nothing"):** Every operation in a transaction must succeed for the transaction to be completed. If even a single operation fails, the entire transaction is rolled back and the database state is left unchanged.

>> **Consistency:** The completion of any transaction brings the database from one valid state to another valid state.

>> **Isolation:** Concurrent transactions do not contend for access to the data and are run as if each transaction executed sequentially.

>> **Durability:** After a transaction is committed, it remains committed.

Data consumers also benefit by receiving immediate access to only the shared data without having to scan the data provider's entire data warehouse to look for the data they need.

Unlimited concurrency

With modern data sharing, shared data can be accessed by large numbers of concurrent data consumers, as shown in Figure 4-5. In contrast, the architecture of traditional data warehouses forces all users to compete for resources, creating a struggle to deliver optimum performance and consistency. Automatic scaling of concurrency takes simultaneous query processing even further in modern data sharing by automating the scaling of additional warehouse compute engines without manual intervention.

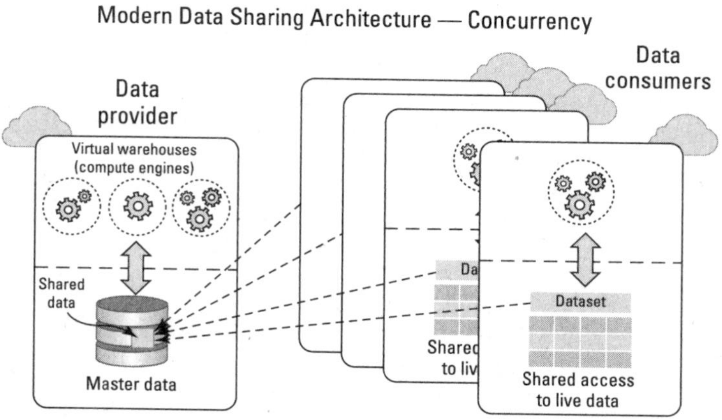

Modern Data Sharing Architecture — Concurrency

FIGURE 4-5: Unlimited concurrency with a modern data sharing architecture.

Using Modern Cloud Data Sharing

Modern cloud data sharing allows access to database tables and views for any user of a modern cloud data warehouse-as-a-service. When a data provider shares part of its data warehouse with a data consumer, the database object and view are all from within the data provider's data warehouse environment.

In addition, a modern cloud data warehouse-as-a-service gives data providers granular control of access to database tables and secure views through *shares.* Data consumers can only query a provider's database if granted access privileges. Once the data provider creates a share, the data consumer can then query the data.

Instant access, without data copying or movement, is made possible because all database objects are maintained and updated only in a modern cloud data warehouse, and orchestrated by its global metadata management services.

How It All Works

As a data provider, the first step to sharing data is to specify what database tables and views to share with specific data consumers. This is done via a data share object, effectively an "empty shell" that houses the references to the actual database and the shared database objects. Data shares are first-class objects in the modern cloud warehouse environment for which it provides a set of data definition language (DDL) commands for creating and managing shares. Commands include create share, alter share, drop share, and others. Access commands include grant and revoke privileges.

Once a share is created, the data provider grants access to the specific database and database objects it shares. The SQL semantics are as follows:

1. **Create the share.** The following example creates an empty share named sales_s:

```
create share sales_s;
```

2. **Add privileges for objects in the share.** Grant usage on the primary object before granting usage on any objects within the primary object. For example, grant usage on a database before granting usage on any schemas contained within the database. Complete all grants for the data share before adding the data sharing consumer(s). The following example grants privileges for the `sales_db` database, the `aggregates_eula` schema, and the `aggregate_1` table to the data-share object:

```
grant usage on database sales_db to
    share sales_s;
grant usage on schema sales_
    db.aggregates_eula to share sales_s;
grant select on table sales_
    db.aggregates_eula.aggregate_1 to
    share sales_s;
```

3. **Confirm the contents of the share:**

```
show grants to share sales_s;
```

4. **Grant access to the share for the intended data consumer(s).** The following example makes the `sales_s` share available to other modern cloud data warehouse environments:

```
alter share sales_s add
    accounts=data_consumerA, data_
    consumerB;
```

`data_consumerA` and `data_consumerB` now can see their individual shared data and can create their databases from the shared data as necessary.

The few preceding steps demonstrate that a data provider can easily share live data with any number of data consumers.

Controlling Access to Shared Data with Secure Views

What if you have sensitive data in your database?

With a modern data warehouse built for the cloud and built for data sharing, you are not limited to sharing entire databases or entire database tables. If portions of a table are subject to strict security and confidentiality policies, sharing the entire table exposes the sensitive data. With a command utility called *secure view*, a modern cloud data warehouse enables you to control access to shared data and avoid security breaches, as shown in Figure 4-6.

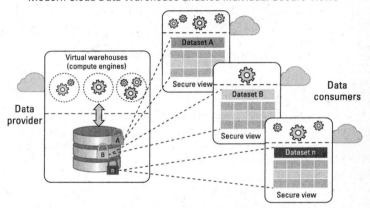

FIGURE 4-6: Secure view in a modern cloud data warehouse allows data providers to protect access to sensitive data.

For example, for online retailers to plan inventory levels, they need to share merchandise and sales data with their distributors. However, the table within the database that contains the sales data also contains sensitive customer ID information, which must be blocked and protected.

To demonstrate how to accomplish this using a secure view, follow the SQL semantics from the previous section to create a data share object, `sales_s` for database `sales_db`. For this example, assume `sales_db` and `sales_s` already exist. The schema for sales_db is named public, within which, table unitsales is constructed as unitsales (customerid, sku, date, qty) and is populated with data.

When you need to plan new inventory with your distributor, you want to provide access to the unit sales data, but not the customer data, which is sensitive. Therefore, a secure view is created from the unitsales table, just for the distributor. The secure view is named distributor_sales_data.

With a modern cloud data warehouse, the steps are accomplished as follows:

1. **Create the secure view.** Assuming that the database and schema are already created and populated with data, the next step is to create a secure view on the unitsales table:

```
create secure view sales_db.
    public.distributor_sales_data as
    select sku, date, qty
    from sales_db.public.unitsales;
```

This logic creates a secure view named, but without the sensitive customerID data. The data included in the view are sku, date, and qty.

2. **In the sales_s share container, add privileges for the secure view:**

```
grant usage on database sales_db to
    share sales_s;
grant usage on schema sales_db.public
    to share sales_s;
grant select on view sales_db.public.
    distributor_
sales_data to
    share sales_s;
```

This logic enables the share (container), sales_s to have privileges for the distributor_sales_data secure view.

3. **Confirm the contents of the share:**

```
desc share sales_s;
```

The user is provided a readout confirmation of the share, sale_s.

4. **Grant the distributor access to the share** (it is assumed the distributor is also a modern cloud-built data warehouse user):

```
alter share sales_s add
    accounts=<distributor_name>;
```

5. **To see your share:**

```
show shares;
```

As the preceding example demonstrates, data providers can easily share data, while controlling data consumers' access to data with a secure view. Sensitive data is protected, and data consumers gain access to non-sensitive data for their own analytics, without the need to copy or move data.

REMEMBER

With unlimited data sharing and multi-tenancy capabilities, modern cloud data sharing extends the capabilities of a built-for-the-cloud data warehouse, enabling organizations to easily forge one-to-one, one-to-many, and many-to-many relationships to share data in new and imaginative ways.

Chapter **5**

Assessing the Impact of Modern Data Sharing

n this chapter, you learn how modern data sharing enables real-time collaboration, which technologies and trends have enabled a modern data sharing architecture, and how modern data sharing can enable organizations to quickly create new business assets from data.

Modern Approaches to Data Collaboration

Traditionally, data sharing has typically meant sharing copies of data, rather than sharing access to the same, live data that doesn't move (see Figure 5-1). This creates a myriad of challenges including:

» Single, point-in-time copies of data sets exist and are quickly outdated or out of sync.

» Multiple versions of the same data exist in different environments, across multiple data silos.

>> No practical single source-of-truth or governance exists for data in the organization.

>> Critical business decisions are made based on outdated, incomplete, or inaccurate data.

>> Version control of multiple data sets becomes an increasingly untenable management burden.

>> Electronic discovery costs escalate when multiple sources of data within and outside an organization must be identified, searched, and produced for litigation support.

>> The potential number of data breaches and accidental data loss/disclosure risks multiply, along with their associated costs, such as breach notifications, credit monitoring services, damage to an organization's brand, customer churn, litigation, forensic analysis, and recovery.

>> Data storage requirements and costs grow exponentially as redundant data is stored in multiple locations within and outside the organization.

Traditional Data Sharing Pain

PROVIDER AND CONSUMER SHARE THE PAIN

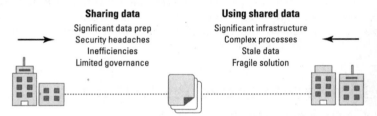

Sharing data	Using shared data
Significant data prep	Significant infrastructure
Security headaches	Complex processes
Inefficiencies	Stale data
Limited governance	Fragile solution

FIGURE 5-1: The difficulties of traditional data sharing methods.

Modern data sharing enables fast, cost-effective, and secure collaboration inside and outside the enterprise by providing data consumers with real-time access to a single copy of the same data. With modern data sharing, data providers can share data using the same modern cloud data warehouse platform they use to run their enterprises.

The Democratization of Computing

Enterprise-grade computing power is everywhere and it's getting even more powerful, faster, and less expensive every day. The cloud has further accelerated this trend, making limitless computing resources easily available at massive scale to any sized enterprise.

With this much power, many analytical computing tasks are now performed directly by business users rather than submitted as queued job requests for IT administrators to perform. Business analysts have the power to run advanced analytics against large data sets. Data scientists can execute predictive analytics and develop machine learning algorithms that serve as the basis for artificial intelligence. Business executives can execute swiftly with up-to-the-minute analytics dashboards, while product management executives achieve faster time to market for new products and services. In short, massive computing power is now within everyone's reach.

Data-Driven Business Decisions

To ensure the most complete view of customers, today's enterprises require a multi-channel approach to gathering data from various channels (such as websites, mobile devices, point-of-sale terminals, call centers, and so on). Traditional data warehouses not only fail when sharing data, but they also perform poorly when needing to uncover meaningful relationships between different forms of data from different channels. The variety of data formats — tables, spreadsheets, and other forms of structured data mixed with JavaScript Object Notation (JSON) and other forms of *semi-structured data* — exacerbates the challenges faced by traditional data warehouse technologies.

TECHNICAL STUFF

Semi-structured data does not conform to the standards of traditionally structured data and includes data generated from newer data sources such as social media sites, clickstreams, mobile devices, and Internet of Things (IoT) devices.

But collecting and analyzing all this data from multiple channels is exactly what successful businesses need. Outcomes from insightful analytics can help organizations better target new products and services. So, it's understandable that enterprises that want to provide data as a service, or as a value-added business asset, are just as interested in delivering access to data quickly and easily so other, non-competing enterprises can benefit.

Growing Opportunities for the Commercialization of Data

By removing traditional barriers of on-premises and cloud data warehouses, modern cloud data sharing introduces at least four new economic opportunities that enable enterprises to share data as packaged and monetized assets, quickly and securely, powering a true data economy:

>> **Data monetization:** Many companies produce and sell data, some of which started more than 70 years ago. Now, with modern data sharing, any company can turn its data, regardless of its size, into a business asset by charging for access to slices of its data warehouse. This low-cost, zero-headache solution enables data companies to immediately meet data consumers' urgent demands for fresh data with up-to-the-minute accuracy, which maintains the highest value for data. Organizations have greater power and platform capabilities to support, move forward, and implement data monetization strategies.

>> **Data sharing with business partners:** Sharing data directly with business partners is not new. But effortless sharing of live data is groundbreaking. Modern cloud data sharing enables

- Enterprises to share data instantly with other enterprises that are part of their business ecosystem — for example, supply chain, distribution, marketing, third-party sales, and so on

- Data consumers to query against live data to mutually benefit both the data consumer and data provider, no matter which enterprise owns the data and no matter which enterprise takes on the role of either the data provider or data consumer

- Business results to be delivered faster from faster execution of analytics based on internal and external data sources that are accessed immediately, without overhead, and at a fraction of the cost of traditional data sharing methods

>> **Breaking down enterprise data silos:** Modern data sharing eliminates data silos strewn across the enterprise and beyond by allowing structured and semi-structured data to be easily stored in a modern cloud data warehouse. Data can be shared seamlessly, without downloading or replication. Systems that were previously siloed can be tightly integrated, without manual integration or the need for data pipelines.

>> **Zero management to reach more data consumers:** Only a modern cloud data warehouse eliminates the traditional and time-consuming methods needed to manage a legacy data warehouse. Because performance is built into the modern data warehouse, there's no infrastructure to tweak, no knobs to turn, and no tuning required. With zero management required, enterprises can pursue more, far-reaching data sharing strategies to target a larger base of data consumers across their organizations, with business partners inside their ecosystem, and with other enterprises as part of the data economy.

Data economy refers to the global supply and demand of data as a currency and a business asset.

Data sharing should exist only as the technology enabler and business model, making it effortless to create a self-service environment. All business arrangements between data providers and consumers are their own.

THOUSANDS OF DATA CONSUMERS — ONE SOURCE OF TRUTH

PlaceIQ aggregates, collects, and anonymizes data from thousands of applications on mobile devices. It then makes the data available for companies that want to target and reach out to mobile consumers based on their location and behavior. PlaceIQ customers may include marketing companies, advertising agencies, and product producers, to name a few.

One data source — thousands of self-service users

PlaceIQ customers execute highly targeted campaigns based on the individual usage and geographic movement of mobile device users. To do so, each PlaceIQ customer may require a unique slice of the data warehouse to qualify potential prospects. The cost and effort of traditional methods made it impossible to effortlessly deliver the data within a self-service business model.

Effective business models — zero-data management

A modern cloud data warehouse, built for data sharing, resolved the challenges faced by PlaceIQ to scale and deliver thousands of individual data consumer subscriptions with governed, secure slices of the data.

PlaceIQ now uses far fewer resources to manage its single source of truth, while enabling its data consumers to self-serve their own data subscription. With modern data sharing, PlaceIQ focuses on developing new use cases for its data which are differentiated and priced accordingly for every customer.

Simplicity for PlaceIQ data consumers

PlaceIQ customers also benefit by having a simple environment to assess shared data before merging it with their own data sets. In doing so, PlaceIQ customers do not have to sort through large amounts of irrelevant data to find the information they desire. Plus, all the data from the modern data warehouse meets common security and certification requirements. PlaceIQ customers are able to blend data sets without compliance issues.

Chapter **6**

Six Steps to Advance Your Business with Modern Data Sharing

N ow that you understand the enormous potential of modern data sharing and the challenges of traditional data sharing methods, it's time to consider the possible impact and benefits of modern data sharing. This chapter outlines six key steps to help you and your enterprise get started with modern data sharing to advance your business:

1. **Uncover data sharing barriers and opportunities.**

   The goal in this step is to gather a snapshot of data sharing requirements within your organization — both now and for the near-term future. You need a firm handle on data flows and work processes already in place to share data.

   When you have this information, focus on identifying the data that has the potential to produce the most value. Ultimately, the objective is to uncover laborious data sharing and data transferring processes that are robbing you of productivity and resources within your IT, data warehouse, and business analytics groups. These barriers create delays in producing business value from data. Identify these barriers and set the stage for easier and faster execution of your data sharing business plans. Here's what to look for:

- **Data:** What types of data must the data warehouse contain? At what rate is new data created? How often will data move into the warehouse?

- **Data flows:** Identify the current data flows in place from your data warehouse to any other organization. Determine the number of organizations. Note which of the data flows are internal (within your organization) and which ones are external.

- **Work processes:** Which teams are currently managing the work processes for data sharing or data transfers? Identify the tools being used, and whether they are extract, transform, and load (ETL) or data replication tools. If your team isn't managing those processes, talk with the appropriate teams to gather their insights as to the level of difficulty they encounter when sharing data.

- **Future time-to-market and time-to-insight objectives:** Know your data sharing needs in the present and near-term future, without regard to your current tools and available expertise. Identify your near-term and future time-to-market goals, highlighting where there is too much latency and where reducing that latency could have significant business value.

2. **Define your role for each use case.** Elevating a corporate initiative to a new level of capability requires a champion to establish the vision and objectives, and to make things happen. Organizational improvement, especially in IT and data warehouse areas, does not happen on its own:

- Identify the use cases for data sharing, both current and future.

- Identify the organizations, internal and external, that must be brought on board. All data sharing relationships have at least two stakeholders — the data provider and the data consumer(s). Be clear about which role your organization will play for each use case. Strive to keep the organizational structure as simple as possible.

- As a data provider, identify and engage your data consumers to have them adopt a similar modern data sharing strategy. This helps to quickly and easily enable live, governed, and secure data sharing capabilities.

- As a data consumer, approach the data provider to influence the adoption of a similar modern data sharing approach.

3. **Confirm that your data warehouse solution can easily and cost-effectively enable modern data sharing.** This step is where the rubber meets the road. To determine if your data warehouse can enable modern data sharing, look for these capabilities:

   - *Data does not move:* Modern data sharing enables data to be shared without any data movement, ETL, or file transfer. This is the lion's share of the cumbersome work required to share data. Eliminating data movement puts you on a better path for limitless data sharing.

   - *Real-time updates:* As a data provider, the value of your data increases with its freshness. The more current your data, the more value your data consumers will perceive and receive from the data you've shared and potentially monetized. As a data consumer, you always want to run analytics on the most up-to-date information.

   - *Individual secure views:* Modern data sharing is not about simply creating access to your entire data warehouse for all your data consumers. It's about having the granular control to easily provide the necessary view of the data as required for each data consumer. Modern data sharing enables one-to-one, one-to-many, and many-to-many data sharing relationships. The tool you choose should give you this flexibility.

   - *Single source of truth with transactional integrity:* As a data provider updates its data, a modern data warehouse ensures that every consumer of the data sees the change as soon as it's committed. This should be possible without any extra labor on the part of the data provider or consumer. Data consumers want this level of integrity, which increases the value of your data.

4. **Implement a proof of concept (PoC).** After investigating data warehouse options, viewing demos, asking questions, and meeting with vendor teams, you should execute a PoC as soon as possible. A PoC is a process of testing a solution to determine how well it serves your needs and meets your success criteria. Think of it as a test drive. Compare the benefits of modern data sharing against traditional data warehouse approaches.

Consider what else you can do above and beyond what you do today with data. If you had a modern, cloud-built data warehouse that enables modern data sharing, what additional business value could the system deliver? You may want to monetize some of your data. How will you accomplish this? When setting up your PoC, list all current and future requirements and success criteria.

For example, if your primary complaint about your current data warehouse is that queries take too long to run, don't focus solely on that issue. Your PoC should validate assumptions about all or most high-value requirements, including ease of migrating your data to the new solution, loading new structured and semi-structured data, running queries, and handling multiple workloads.

5. **Create an outreach plan.** Outline the steps necessary to engage your data consumers. Because modern data sharing can facilitate one-to-one, one-to-many, and many-to-many data sharing relationships, you must communicate the value of your data and the benefits data consumers can expect to receive.

6. **Execute — demonstrate time-to-market and time-to-value improvements to your business stakeholders.** After completing your PoC, demonstrate the benefits of modern data sharing to your stakeholders. Estimate time savings and related cost savings for your enterprise as the data provider and/or the data consumer. Demonstrate the improvements in productivity your enterprise will gain and, if applicable, forecast the revenue potential for monetizing your data. You should be able to develop a complete picture of the ROI potential for modern data sharing and a modern cloud-built data warehouse. You will then be well on your way to taking data sharing to new levels of capabilities and opportunities for your enterprise.